CW00971799

Saint George
& the Dragon

written by JIM FOREST and
illustrated by VLADISLAV ANDREJEV

ST VLADIMIR'S SEMINARY PRESS • YONKERS • NEW YORK • 2011

The dragon had been given no name by the local people. Generation after generation it was known simply as "the dragon." People spoke of it in nervous whispers, as if the dragon might be just around the corner, listening.

Many in the town had seen the beast at a distance. Though no two people agreed about every detail of the dragon's appearance, everyone knew it was much larger than a horse, was covered with emerald green scales, breathed fire when enraged, and could speak with a voice that had the authority of a king. Its home was in a lake in which no one ever swam or fished. It had an awful smell. Children were warned, "If ever your nose tells you that there are dead fish rotting nearby, run for home as fast as your feet will carry you! It isn't fish you're smelling. It's the dragon."

FOR YEARS BEYOND COUNTING the people had lived in peace with the dragon, at least a peace of sorts. Each week, they brought it two sheep. By nightfall all that was left of the sheep were fragments of bloodstained bone. More than a hundred sheep per year was a costly gift, but the alternative was to have a dragon at war with the town and all the people living round about. There were ancient stories of the dragon entering the town, killing people and burning houses.

The sheep were traditionally brought to the dragon's killing field, as it was known, by the town shepherd and his son. On one fateful day the boy hadn't been quick enough in leaving the sheep. Not only were the sheep eaten, but so was the shepherd's son. From that day onward the dragon would no longer accept only sheep. There had to be a child as well.

What were the people to do? No one dared fight the dragon. Who could hope to defeat a fire-breathing monster? Even a crowd of men felt despair in imagining combat with a creature whose scales were said to be hard as diamonds. And all could easily imagine what the dragon would do to the town if they resisted. "Better to lose twelve children a year than to lose everyone and everything," reasoned the king.

AND SO IT WAS that lots were drawn each month. The names of all the children from twelve to eighteen years old were placed in a bowl. By the king's own hand, each month a single name was taken out of the bowl— the next child to be given to the dragon.

Every time the king had to reach into the bowl of names, his hand trembled. No child was excused from the draw. What if he should pull out the paper with the name of his only child, his precious daughter Elizabeth? But luck seemed to be on his side. Months passed, then years, and each time some other name was on the paper he unfolded. Other parents howled in grief, but the king and queen were spared the loss of their child.

In another month Elizabeth would celebrate her nineteenth birthday. Her name would no longer be placed in the bowl. Only one more month!

The day came. The king reached into the bowl, begging all the gods to keep his fingers away from his daughter's name. But the gods were not listening. When his shaking hand unfolded the paper, on it was the name "Elizabeth."

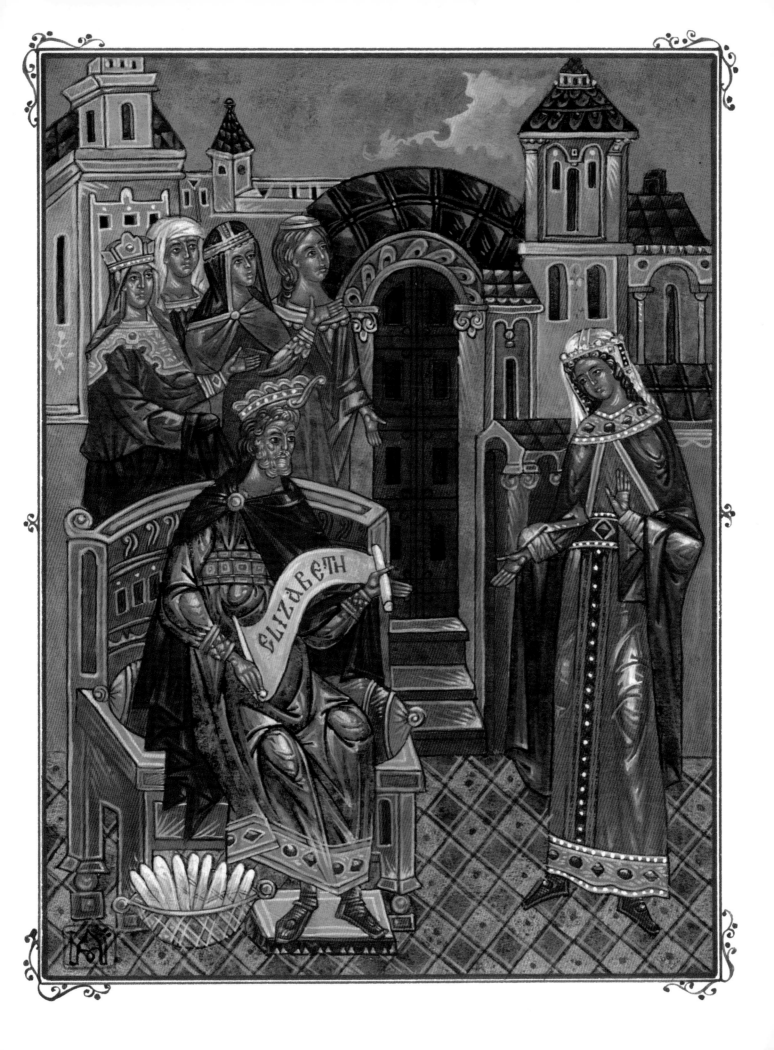

NOT ONLY THE KING AND QUEEN wept as
Elizabeth led the two sheep to the killing field. Elizabeth
was loved by everyone in the town. When she sang, her
voice was like a nightingale's. When anyone was sick,
she was always at the bedside giving care.

Elizabeth herself seemed at peace as she said goodbye
at the town gates, embracing in turn each person.
"Perhaps the dragon has lost interest in eating people,"
she told her parents, "or perhaps he's died of indiges-
tion."

But in her heart of hearts, she felt no hope. So many of
her friends had died in the years she was growing up.
No one had ever dared oppose the dragon. She felt sorry
for her parents, sorry for her town. But for the sake of
all the people she loved, Elizabeth hid her terror.

She led the two sheep away from the town and never
looked back, even when she heard the sound of the
gates closing behind her. "Let no one see my fear," she
said to herself. "May heaven give me courage and help
me!"

SO BUSY WAS ELIZABETH repeating her desperate prayer that she wasn't aware of the man on horseback until she had reached the swamp's edge. By now she could see the dragon gazing at her with burning eyes as it waded toward her. But the unexpected sound of a horse neighing made her turn her face.

It would have amazed Elizabeth to see anyone near the killing field, but here was an armored knight with a lance that seemed twice the length of the white horse he was riding.

THE DRAGON'S FURIOUS GAZE shifted.
It opened it jaws and a river of fire exploded toward the knight. Elizabeth screamed.

Heedless of the flames, the knight charged forward. Because smoke filled the battlefield, Elizabeth could hardly see the struggle, even though it took place all around her. There was the reek of the dragon, the smell of fire, the thudding noise of the horse's hooves and the shout of the knight, "In Christ's name, submit or perish!" Then came a great silence.

ELIZABETH THOUGHT SURELY the knight had lost his life. No other result seemed possible. Yet as the breeze carried the smoke away, the knight stood unharmed on the ground, his horse at his side and his lance in the dragon's neck.

The dragon was not dead—the wound had not been fatal. Yet fire was no longer issuing from its mouth. The stunned creature seemed as docile as a well-mastered dog.

"SIR, WHO ARE YOU?" Elizabeth asked.

"I am George, a Christian knight."

"What brings you here and what gives you courage to do battle with a dragon?"

"I am a follower of Jesus Christ, my lady. He has sent me into the world to win him followers. He would not allow me to stand by and watch a wicked beast take your life."

Elizabeth had sometimes heard rumors of someone called "Jesus Christ," but in her own town the people still believed in the old gods.

"Sir, tell me of this Jesus and how it is he gives you the strength to battle dragons. None of the gods our people worship have given us such bravery."

"THERE IS ONLY ONE GOD, not many," George told her, "but in God's oneness exists a Trinity—Father, Son and Holy Spirit." George made the sign of the cross on his body. "Through a virgin named Mary, the Son of God became man and was named Jesus. He taught all who would listen how to live in the kingdom of God. He healed the sick and even raised the dead, but finally the rulers decided he was a threat and had him killed, nailing him to a cross." George pointed at the cross on his shield. "They thought they were finished with him, but death could not keep him a captive. On the third day he rose from the grave. Life conquered death. This is what makes his followers stronger than dragons."

"Please, sir, come meet my parents. You must explain all this to them," begged Elizabeth.

THE DRAGON MOANED, frightening Elizabeth. "But what are we to do with the dragon?" she asked.

"Take your belt, tie it around his neck, and lead him back to the town," George replied. "From now on he will be the town's guardian instead of its enemy."

Elizabeth did as she was told. The wounded creature followed her as if it were a dog on a leash. She and the dragon led the way, with George and his horse walking beside them, along with the two sheep.

ON THE TOWN WALLS, Elizabeth could see her parents and neighbors. There were shouts of joy as the gates were opened, though at first none dared come close to her as she had the dragon at her side.

George spoke. "Good people, please don't be afraid. In Jesus Christ's name the dragon has been made peaceful. In the years to come he will be your guardian. Forgive him the harm he did in the past. Heal his injury and let him be your servant."

THE KING WAS THE FIRST to step forward, embracing his daughter, then greeting George. "You have saved not only my daughter's life but also the lives of many others who would have been given to the dragon in time to come. How can we ever reward you? What gift would you accept? We gladly offer you every coin and jewel we possess."

"MY LORD," GEORGE RESPONDED,
"I seek no such treasure. I only wish for your salvation.
Let me teach you and all who live here the story and
teaching of Jesus. He gives his followers the strength
to overcome dragons. All I ask is that you prepare
yourselves for baptism."

"So be it," said the king. "So be it!"

THE END

THE REAL SAINT GEORGE

True stories become streamlined into legends and legends become compressed into myths.

The real Saint George never saw a dragon nor did he rescue a princess in distress. We are not even sure he had a horse or possessed a lance or sword. It is possible he was a farmer. The name "George" means tiller of the soil. For this reason Saint George is a patron saint of agriculture, herds, flocks, and shepherds.

A Christian convert who was born late in the third century after Christ and died early in the fourth century, Saint George was one among many martyrs of the early Church. The word "martyr" is Greek for "witness." A martyr is someone who dies for Christ and whose death bears witness to his faith.

What made George a saint especially loved and remembered by the Church was the completely fearless manner in which he openly proclaimed his faith during a period of fierce persecution when many other Christians were hoping not to be noticed. According to one ancient account, Saint George went to a public square and announced, "All the gentile gods are devils. My God made the heavens and is the true God."

For this Saint George was arrested, cruelly tortured and finally beheaded. The probable date of his martyrdom is April 23, 303, in the town of Nicomedia (in the northwest of modern Turkey). His body was later brought to his birthplace, Diospolis, later known as Lydda, and today as Lod in modern-day Israel. His courageous witness led to the conversion of many and gave renewed courage to others already baptized.

Saint George was one of the early victims of the anti-Christian persecution ordered by the Emperor Diocletian that began in February of the year 303. Churches were destroyed and biblical texts burned. All Roman subjects were ordered to make ritual sacrifices to Rome's gods. Those who refused risked severe punishment. Many were sent into exile as slave laborers in quarries and mines in Egypt and Palestine. Thousands were tortured and many executed. Finally, in 311, the attack ended. With Diocletian in retirement and the emperor Galerius critically ill and close to death, Galerius published an edict of toleration allowing Christians to restore their places of worship and to worship in their own way without interference, provided they did nothing to disturb the peace.

Previous page: icon of St George, taken from the Church of St George, in the village of Staro Nagoricane, Macedonia.

This page, from left to right: 1) St George and the Dragon. Novgorod, ca. 1450–1500; 2) St George and the Dragon. 3) St George and the Dragon. Russian icon, early 15th c., Tretyakov Gallery, Moscow. Photo: Scala/Art Resource, New York.

Persecution ended, but the memory of those eight years of suffering would never be forgotten. George was one of the saints whose witness remained fresh. His icon hung in more and more churches. As centuries passed, he became the patron saint not only of many churches and monasteries but even of cities and whole countries.

In early icons, made in the centuries before the legend of the dragon became attached to his name, we see him dressed as a soldier and holding the cross of martyrdom.

Perhaps Saint George was in the army, but it may be that he is shown in military clothing because he so perfectly exemplifies the qualities that Saint Paul spoke of in his letter to the Ephesians, in which he calls on Christ's followers to wear the helmet of salvation and the armor of righteousness, to be girded with truth, to clad their feet in the gospel of peace, to possess the sword of the Spirit which is the word of God, and to protect themselves from the devil's flaming arrows with the shield of faith (Ephesians 6:10–17).

Such symbolic use of a Roman soldier's equipment does not rule out the possibility that Saint George was in fact a soldier. People from every class and profession were drawn to the gospel, soldiers among them. George may have been one of these.

It was only in later centuries that the dragon legend emerged. It has been told in many variations, but in its most popular form it concerns a dragon living in a lake who was worshiped by the unbaptized local people, who in their fear sacrificed their children to appease the creature. Finally it was the turn of the king's daughter, Elizabeth, to be sacrificed. While she was going toward the dragon to meet her doom, Saint George appeared riding a white horse. He prayed to the Father, Son, and Holy Spirit, then transfixed the dragon with his lance. Afterward Elizabeth led the vanquished creature into the city.

According to the *Golden Legend,* a collection of saints' lives written by Blessed James de Voragine about 1260 AD, the wounded monster followed Elizabeth "as if it had been a meek beast and debonair." Refusing a reward of treasure, George called on the local people to be baptized. The king agreed, also promising to build and maintain churches, honor the clergy, faithfully attend religious services, and be generous to the poor.

From the point of view of history, the dragon story is apocryphal. Yet when you think about it, what better way to symbolize the evil that George actually confronted and defeated than to portray it in the form of a fire-breathing dragon? Saint George fought and was victorious over an adversary which terrified most of the people of his time. We can understand the dragon as representing anything that makes us afraid.

The white horse Saint George rides in the icon, a graceful creature as light as air and as fearless as his rider, represents the courage God gave to George as he challenged evil. It is the courage God gives to any Christian facing martyrdom.

In many versions of the icon, the lance Saint George holds is shown resting lightly

St George and the Dragon; Elizabeth leads the dragon with her belt. Russian, Novgorod School, early 14th c.

in his open hand, meaning that it is the power of God, not the power of man, that overcomes evil.

Notice how thin the lance is and that in many Saint George icons there is a small cross at the top of the lance. The icon stresses that it is not with weapons of war that evil is overcome but with the power of the Cross, the life-giving Cross that opens the path to the resurrection.

Similarly, even in battle with the dragon, Saint George's face shows not a trace of anger, hatred, or anxiety. His tranquil face reminds us of Christ's commandment that his followers must love their enemies.

In many versions of the icon, the hand of the Savior is extended from heaven in a sign of blessing. This

detail is a reminder that whatever we do bears good fruit only if it is God's will and has God's blessing.

In more detailed versions of the icon there are scenes before and after the battle with the dragon. Sometimes a castle is in the background, from which Elizabeth's parents watch all that happens.

Some icons depicting Saint George's victory show Elizabeth leading the wounded dragon on a leash made of her belt or scarf—a victory of life over death, similar to Christ's resurrection.

Bringing a wounded but still living dragon back to the town, in its new role of guardian, provides us with a powerful symbol of the conversion rather than the destruction of enemies. The final fruit of Saint George's combat with the dragon is neither victory over a monster nor financial reward for successful combat but bringing unbelieving people to conversion and baptism.

Finally, as is the case with any icon, the Saint George icon is not a decoration, but an invitaiton to prayer. It belongs in the icon corner of any home where courage is sought—courage to be a faithful disciple of Christ; courage to fight rather than flee from whatever dragons we meet in life; courage to live in such a way that others may be made more aware of Christ and the life he offers to us.

LIBRARY OF CONGRESS CATALOGING-IN-PUBLICATION DATA

Forest, Jim (James H.)
  Saint George & the dragon / written by Jim Forest and illustrated by Vladislav Andrejev.
    p. cm.
  ISBN 978-0-88141-373-1 (alk. paper)
I. Andrejev, Vladislav, 1938- , ill. II. Title: Saint George and the dragon.
PZ8.1.F78Sai 2011
398.2—dc23

2011017396

The publication
of this book was made
possible by a
generous donation from
Bob & Connie Abodeely.

ST VLADIMIR'S SEMINARY PRESS
575 Scarsdale Road, Yonkers, New York 10707
1-800-204-2665
www.svspress.com

book & cover design: Amber Schley Iragui
typeset in Goudy Thirty

PRINTED IN CHINA